The Scarlet Thread in the Cloth of Time

Stephen B. Machnik

**Library and Archives Canada
Cataloguing in Publication**

All rights reserved. No part of this book may be used or reproduced in any manner whatsoever without the prior written permission of the publisher except for minor extracts embodied in critical articles or reviews.

Machnik, Stephen B.
    The Scarlet Thread in the Cloth of Time

ISBN: 978-1-7383111-0-1   HARDCOVER
ISBN: 978-1-7383111-1-8   PAPERBACK
ISBN: 978-1-7383111-2-5   EBOOK

    I. Title   1. Poetry

© Rain on Grass Publishers, Montreal, QC, Canada

Contact publisher at:
sm at rainongrass dot com

Book cover design and photo by the author
Typesetting by L.B. Word Works, Victoria, BC, Canada

Contents

Introduction   v
Dedication..vi

1960   1
The End 1
By Kayak... 1
Song of Love 8

1991   9
Made In His Image 9
Why?... 10
Homeroom... 11

2003   12
Jerusalem 12

2004   15
The Scarlet Thread in the Cloth of Time 15
Does Not Israel Have the Right to Be?............. 17
The Heart 18
In Chaldean Lands 19
The Life of Man 19

2005   20
Passover 20
In a Whisper of Time.. 25
The Pen 26
The Desert Manna 27
Montmorency Falls 27

2006   29

   The Hidden Battle 29
   What? Evolution! 31
   The Deranged Birds 32
   Wendy 34
   The Absolute 37
   The Crows 37

2008   39

   Green Olive Tree 39
   A Note from the Future 41
   On Mount Sinai's Tortured Height 42
   The Five Talents 43
   Interchangeable Nature 44
   The Acacia Box 46
   Word Construction 49
   The Native American Woman 50
   I Want to Take Refuge in Earth 52

2009   54

   The Tree 54
   The Train Station 56
   I Swallowed the Bitter Pill 56

2011   57

   Jasper 57

2012   60

   The Three Types of Fusion Process 60
   A Fine Mist in the Night 62
   The Cardinal's Message 63

2013   64
Two Mating Dragonflies 64

2014   65
The Mystical Messianic Turns of the Wheel .. 65
Principles 71
Cpl. Cirillo 71
On the Plaines 72

2015   74
As Time Goes By 74
The Magnificent Chariot 75
By Way of the Land Laid Waste 76

2016   77
Memorial for Stan 77
Eldercare Entertainment at the Speed of Light
.... 78
Narrative in Transition 80
My Love is like a Red Red Rose 83

2017   85
The Irish Rover 85
Clarity 89

2019   90
Esquimalt 90

2021   92
The Aftermath 92
All Hands on Deck 93
Bug Book 93
No Never I Be 94
The Muse 96

2022   97

    Events in my Life Today 97
    My Valentine 98
    Cat Man Do 99
    Elizabeth 99
    Gold Dust at My Feet 102
    Poem at Solstice 103

2023   104

    Mourning Dove 104
    Articles previously posted in The Montreal
        Review 2023 – 24 106
    Let Us Make Man in Our Image - צלם, After Our
        Likeness – דמות (Gen 1:26) 106
    A Male Bias in the New Testament? 115

Introduction

Stephen B. Machnik published *The Tree of Life* with Wipf & Stock in Eugene, OR., in 2021. He has also published articles in the Montreal Review. Machnik has a master's degree in theology from Concordia University in Montreal, Quebec, a B.A. from Bishops, and four years at the Ecole des Beaux Arts in Montreal. Poems by his wife, Wendy Mellor Machnik and his son Jasper are included from 1991, and by his granddaughter Vienna in 2022. Jasper worked as a DJ at the Foufounes Electriques in Montreal from 2002 to 2020. Wendy continues to work as a crisis intervention worker.

Dedication

This book is dedicated to all those who feel that there is a spirit within, a spirit who and which is above and beyond, and is capable of helping and taking us out of our normal human condition, and which makes all things possible.

1960

The End

The sun was kind
to me that day
warm it splashed
on cool green grass
it gave me happiness
when i had none
a peaceful laughter
on the bottom rung
He gave me all that
and more.

                                                  1964.6

By Kayak

Sun crashing down
light blue sky
lissom clouds
lay lengthwise
we set out
paddled and pried
two bottles of rum
four hundred cigarettes
and some other supplies
booming waves
drummed in our ears
then lay still
a ghostly heron sadly soars
into our firelit sky
voluminous
we specks below
no tiddledeedum

for those on the run
glide out
set course
with the morning sun
sing
no fear
water deep clear
brain bleary and eighty-proof

and on and alone
and woebegone
bridges and breakers go by
so many miles more
then eat, sleep and be damned
and sleep
and once more we ran
and rested
strutted before
the fair-haired gentry
citing our woes of having to flee
to wrestle the white tossed way
into a south wind and up "the Gut"
to another fire

we lay all night
under canvas
plastered by rain
in the distance
a barn door cracked
intermittently like a .303
bacon and eggs and the bottles almost dry
and we come to a ferry landing
where land locked mermaids
serve hot coffee
and nature threw a party
and the wind and the waves

and all hell broke loose
and you're alone
pulling for your
sweet f'ing life
telling God you'd been a pretty bad boy
but you'll be a helluva lot better from now on
and land,
a sweet crummy wave beaten rock gnarled island
that smells like eau de cologne
and looks like paradise
the sun's streaming through the glistening leaves
and a rainbow steeps the gray skies in pastel
a big bloody bonfire
and man you're going to have a wet warm sleep
    tonight

across the settled waters
Plattsburgh bristles black and bright
a big police launch rumbles eerily by
the spotlight picking you off
at 200 yards
and quiet
but its wake comes back to haunt you by and by
the trees flicker and glow by the fire
and way high the stars kinda stretch your mind
and time floats by
morning comes
bright and clear
your food's running out
sleeping bag sorta got burnt
and you got a hankering for
some crummy american beer

but you're almost there
along the way a craggy island
and rock

it shoots right outa the water
like it wanted to cleave the sky
your boat batters forth
knifing the waves
and thudding in the furrows
so like God help us
but i don't know why
but we're here
in this au sable river
and wild
blue heron drift lazy like by
and dragonflies nestle on our bow
and crazy mallards flap madly all over the place
and you're the only souls in creation
except for this big
black bastard of a 1913
Hudson and Delaware rail bridge
that was riveted all to hell
and protruded in and out of the wilderness
like a lost soul
in the garden of eden

a while latter the land broadens out
the water gets kinda rough
and you pass a highway
look around the river bend
a chasm churns in agony
stash the boats
grab the bags
and you're on the road
and on the bum
and town
hick town
come in a cadillac no less
and thank you sir
and much obliged

and walk around like a God forsaken
nuclear creation
sleep on somebody's back lawn
seems like not so long
then people bustling all around
buy some milk, beer, cheese, and bread
so you're broke
and gone

open water once more
wind nil
sun searing down
and skin stretched leather-tight
water liquid glass
prow bleeding through
waves roll lazy so
now and then
slither a thin pool over their crest
surface film that drapes and wallows
smooth
vast
penetrating
blue
deep blues
dire foreboding
black blue
pale blue
and fluffy white
and shallow green blues, grey blues
pink blues, orange blues, red blues
fluorescent blue
and black
and nightlights
and bow lights
port lights, stern lights
and fishing lights

and light the paper Andre or we'll be mowed down
and black
infinite black
rolling blacks
expansive blacks
and jutting blacks
and black walls
ominously massive
closing – closing
in-shout, break out, rout
pull pry
toes curled
head drumming and nothing
nothing but the cool night air
sweetening
your dry rasping breath
and the imagery of beings below
the lifeless drops
without a sparkle
feeding the vortex your paddle made
denizens of the deep
bleary eyed in their watery shell
registering the presence
of a slow plodding phantom
overhead
waiting for a disruption
in its smooth flowing path

then the long-deadened grind
as the plywood planking scrapes the rounded rocks
and fire
a long agonizing
feeble flickering
finger burning
watery eyed

flame
that bursts into a white-hot inferno
but it's fire
a positive print of negative development
a warming
life-giving
bed of light
that lures two lost souls
wandering in a watery wilderness
into this nest of companionship
a return to the womb
that snuggles
and secures
and lightens heavy hearts
and lets minds communicate
without inhibitions
without obligations
simply peacefully free

and so on
all night long
every little flame
a fantastic revelation
every glowing log
an exposé
a slow atom by atom
exposé
until with its last flickering gasp
it dies
into the crumbling dust
the morning wind
blows cool over the dark waters
a last spiral of smoke
curls into the brittle grey skies
and we lie sprawled around a bed of ashes.

          Summer 1964

Song of Love

she is the early spring sun
warm after thunder showers
her skin is a velvet meadow land
rising and falling in sweet fragrant scent
her eyes are the dark shadows in the valley
deep and unknown
her hair is the laughter of the tumbling brook
skimming the yellow sand
her teeth are drops of dew
that garnish the wildflower
her lips are the blood red poppy
that sip sweet nectar
her voice is a southerly gust
rustling a burning bush
her laughter is the trill
of a mockingbird
ecstatic and endearing
her throat is the smooth bough
of the silver birch
curving gently upwards
her tears are the mist in the valley
of melancholy sadness
her arms are the branches
of the weeping willow
her breasts two wild roses
blooming in the wind.

1965

1991

Made In His Image

A mirror fell from heaven
It lay shattered on the floor
I gathered bits together
My hands were raw and sore
My heart was raw from crying
And hope, there was no more
The emptiness surrounded me
Pain pierced me to the core

O Lord my God and Saviour
My soul is bruised and bound
Each ache and passion in me
Lies broken on the ground
I turned my heart from you
I thought I knew the way
How foolish of me Jesus
Please come to me I pray

At last, my child you call Me
Your voice is My delight
The task you ask is easy
Relax, I'll put things right
The pieces were all broken
They were soiled, where could I run?
He thoughtfully reviewed them
Slowly placed them into one

My heart was growing calmer
He smiled lovingly at me
His eyes they shone so clearly
His voice spoke tenderly
My touch has sealed the fractures
My stripes have healed the wounds
My blood, My life has washed you clean
Your heart is now brand new

Behold your image daughter
How precious is the sight
For this is how I made you
So beautiful and bright
Go forth my little darling
My hand is holding you
I never will forsake you
For I am the Shepherd of your life

O how I love my Saviour
For He's tender and He's good
Yes, His Spirit burns within me
For in my place, He stood
He suffered for me sisters (and brothers)
He cried and died for me
My Friend, my King, dear Saviour
You have truly set me free.
                    Wendy Mellor Machnik 1991.06

Why?

Dreams and images sailing by
what do I believe?
Is my heart a sordid place?
Only because I let you
walk all over me
I was down but never out

and now here I am
trembling but standing firm
I have a shining sword in my hand
it glimmers in the Sonlight
and now you are afraid
Why?

                                      Wendy Mellor Machnik

Homeroom

20/40/8. Grab my binder and run!
Streaking through the hall saying "this is how it's done"
Running past a teacher like I was in a marathon
Hitting everybody as I go along
The bell is ringing, so I make a dive
Hit the floor, slide through the door, I'm lucky I'm alive!
Jumping over desks to make it to my seat
Gosh, I hope my English is all complete,
Try to sit down but my seat isn't there
Should have known that my friend always hides my chair.
I stand at attention to hear the anthem play
Homeroom is over; that's how I start my day![1]

      Jasper Machnik. Hudson High, Secondary I

---

[1] Reprinted from Fledglings '91, 15th edition. 1991. Lakeshore School Board.

2003

Jerusalem

I – The Holy City

"If I forget you, O Jerusalem"
how can I forget?
Your memory is not mine,
it's part of every man, whether
your song stirred our sleeping hearts
in some distant land, or else
we stumbled upon your upturned face
and troubled you in our slumber.
How could I forget?
Your walls will remind me.
Even as your stones reminded Abraham
before he drew his knife.
Like wisdom, "you stand on top of the high hill
beside the way, where the paths meet
you cry out by the gates." [2]
You know our dreams, our strategies
even before we approach.
Our thoughts are not ours, you have already
absorbed them. You stand quietly by the gate
to meet us. And if by grace we know you are there
You receive us as a friend at the table.
You prepare a feast, even in the presence of the enemy
you pour your best wine
you call your servants
to attend to our simplest ways
how could we not be overjoyed!

---

[2] Proverbs 8

II – Israel: The People

How could I forget you, Israel?
You are not land
you're a person masquerading
partly recognizable
and partly waiting to be recognized.
A Bride to be presented by the Father.
You pretend to be old and wearied
of all our anxieties. Your face
hides in the creases of the land.
You pretend to be young and
full of expectations
and in your exuberance
you can't imagine why you would be hated.
Nothing makes sense
How could the Bride be called
and the wedding becomes a funeral?
Your Spouse waits
for you to step out in your radiance
Your Maker comes to court
and Love's enemy knows
that your consummation
is his perdition.

III – Israel: A Proclamation

Step out Israel
Step to the expectant rhythm of creation's travail
Step to the dance of your Maker
Knowing that you are splendid in your beauty
Knowing that the trees and fields will clap their
    hands
and lambs will roll over in their rejoicing.
He who calls you waits
waiting for you to proclaim

the words of your own awesome calling.
Speak. Words of proclamation, words
not of reason, dangling on the smoke of men's dreams
but exclamations of prophetic expectation
of a Bride to her Lover.
Speak Israel, proclaim
My Love, my Love, I called, did you not hear?
My Love, I came, I danced, did you not see me in my beauty?
My Love, it's me, the one you hoped for!
And
I will be undeterred by all that had passed before.

      Jerusalem, Yom Kippur, 2003.10.7

2004

The Scarlet Thread
in the Cloth of Time

Somewhere there is a scarlet thread
that weaves through all of time
sometimes we glimpse its passage red
and trace its bloodied line
but mostly the cloth appears just that
as cloth, and nothing more
its folds collapse in furrows soft
into the recesses of the unborn

Sometimes we connect as we join
with other human beings, and some primal
faintly mythic dream stirs us
to believe that we were meant to be re-membered
and then the purpose recedes
even as we grab at the threads, hoping
believing, but the body has by itself removed
through an aperture unforeseen

I want to look back and believe
in holy grails and holy visions
I want to look ahead and hope
that the impossible will happen
that purpose will plant itself like cornstalk
on the highway on the outskirts of Dreadville
But it feels like it won't work

It feels like cloth that just keeps
folding and unraveling and conforming
to the body of its desire
you can hold it up and make it hang
but all that you've done is prolong its time
and you know that eventually it'll collapse and do
all that it wants to, which was to draw around
and keep a body warm, could you imagine otherwise?

And yet it's not for us to throw off the banner
the hope. If not for us who are near
then there are those from afar who will gather up
the same bundle of coarse raw threads
noticing here and there that some have a certain appeal
the determined red among the sage
will weave itself back into the spindles of time
the scarlet will find a way where there is a will

We know it will, we can trace its weave through time
what we don't know is where it will find its way
through our own hearts, and will we let it
or will it gather other threads and warp and woof and
    weave
and find its way around the impassive and immovable
stones of our unbending rules?
Will it work its way over the stubble of our shortcom-
    ings?
Will we let it persist so that even our grave clothes
will walk out when they're called?

So this is the miracle of the scarlet thread
it has a life of its own there are those who've said
for where you will follow its intricate way
its pattern apparent appears as it's played
and this is the answer to the sincere heart
one beat calls and the other remarks
and this I believe if the word is true
it goes out to create the other one too.

                                                                   2004.04.8

Does Not Israel Have the Right to Be?

Does not Israel have the right to be
the question falls like petals from the tree
the answer lies in the heap of broken leaves
the pattern cries out from the grave

Not more than seven decades ago
England severed the vineyard's flow
and the tree stood naked
while its sap congealed
at Europe's gates

It would have been nice if Jerusalem
had stood on England's green and
pleasant land, but it could never be
It stands a lonely outpost
by a shriveled desert tree
buried by bones, words, swords and debris

Britain held the tide, she claims
crippled by contractual demands
and messianic dreams
for a fortnight until

the fourteenth and then she
sailed clean on HMS Euryalus

On the ides of May
the drawn swords of the five Arab kings
swarmed – the honey jar
but by curious fate
the bees stand firm
and this time the nectar holds

For a moment – Hope – Hatikva
and time stands still in Aijalon
centuries of prophecy crash abruptly
and shudder against the wall of what's happening
the waves reverberate against our modern shores
the seas roll over the dead once more
until the unseen hand withdraws
and we are left wondering
at who and how and why and
we are left with ourselves.

            2004.05.27

The Heart

When the heart with
pointed wings
to love lays strife
it turns upon its yearning
while it reaches
for air
for flight

The bird its nest
prepares
with beak and spit
its lair

takes of its cloak
to clothe its young

                                    2004.12.18

In Chaldean Lands

In Chaldean lands
there lived a man
Abram was his name
Called by God
to leave his home
he went with no complaint.

The Life of Man

The life of Man
is like the Word
The head, the heart
the feet

Walked out of Ur
Walked through reeds
Crowned by a thorny Tree
A tree that in the
garden grew
One for Life
and the other to rue

We walk where
we know not how
emboldened by
our dreams.

                                    2004.12

2005

Passover

Passing through
Hebrew
Passing through the land

From Ur to Haran
Abram passes through Canaan to Shechem
under the terebinth tree of Moreh
next to the smoking oven
where entered the covenant parts

Jacob passes through the flock
all the spotted, speckled, and mottled
he crosses over Euphrates to Gilead
passing over Jordan
passing over Jabbok
and crosses through Pineal limping
even into Egypt; as well
Joseph went through all of Egypt

The Lord passes through
as the Angel of Death passes through
passing through the first born as he lays
but the Lord will Passover the door
the door with the bloodied lintel
and stay the destroyer

The first born through the womb passing through
His glory passes by
pillar of fire, pillar of cloud
angel of fire, angel of God
passing through the sea

passing before, passing behind
His glory passes by
to Pharaoh a darkness – to Israel a light

The cloud covered the tent
and the glory of the Lord from within the cloud
filled the Tabernacle
The trumpet of Jubilee shouts forth
on the tenth of the seventh
a day of covering

Passing by Edom
through Moab
into all the kingdoms
to the heights of Pisgah
crossing over Jordan
like a consuming fire

He passes before
passing over dry ground
where water ran upwards
standing in a heap by Zaretan

The Spirit of the Lord came upon Jephthah
he was a breakthrough man
he rose up passing over Gilead
passing through Manasseh
passing through Mizpeh of Gilead
to take the Ammonites

David passes over Kidron past the Olive Trees
the whole countryside wept aloud
as the people passed by
by way of the wilderness
and he comes towards Moriah
the Lord passes by

passes by Elijah
(the wind, the shaking, the stillness)
Elisha passes by the Shunammite
and turns into the upper room

Passing out of Persia
the Spirit passes through
by a proclamation of Cyrus
according to Jeremiah
for the rebuilding of Jerusalem
Nor would the memory of Purim
fail to be passed down
to their descendants

He pushes by his inheritance
furious with the high places

A thousand years pass as a day
and as for man his days are like grass
the wind passes over him and he is gone

Pass by the foolish woman

The Winter is past
scarcely had I passed
when I found the one I love
dropping liquid myrrh
but my beloved is gone

Pass through Judah
so will the Lord of hosts defend Judah
He passes over
go through, go through the gates
The harvest is past
the summer is ended
and we are not saved
They passed between the parts thereof

like the covenant
only to stir trouble
the slaves were not released

Go through the midst of Jerusalem
mark the hearts that sigh for iniquity
a sword goes through the land

Pass by the dry bones

For seven months the search party
the passing through party
passes through to bury
the multitude in the Valley of Hamon Gog

Pass through the waters
pass through the waters
I can no longer pass through
they have over-flown me
so even the Sea that is Dead is alive

No stranger shall pass through her
(the Beautiful City) anymore
I will not pass by Israel anymore
they will break out and pass through the gate
go out – the king will pass before you
the Lord is at your head

O Judah keep your appointed feasts
keep your vows
for the wicked shall no more pass through you
they are utterly cut off
I have caused their iniquity to pass from you
the unclean spirit will pass out of the land

Note it well
that it's not mere chance
that Hebrew and Passing
are of the same branch[3]

So wherever you wander
in the trail of same
remember God's plowshares
who turned under His Name

And what we behold
by the eye of the heart
was interred by the Maker
ere centuries apart

And all of this has come to us now
because of Passover in ancient land
When Hebrew people
through the water passed through
and birthed witness
to God's hand in man.[4]

Passover 2005

---

[3] Eber: עֵבֶר the great-grandson of Shem, son of Noah, the first Semite Hebrew: עִבְרִי the derivative of Eber. He passed: עָבַר or passing

[4] Gen: 12:6, 30:32, 32:22, 41:41, Exo 12:23, 13:21, 40:34, Le 25:9, Deu 3:27, Jos 3:16, Jud 11:1, 2Sam 15:23, 1Kin 19:12, 2Kin 4:8, 2Ch 36:23, Est 9:28, Psa 78:62, 90:4, Pro 9:13, Song 5:5, Isa 62:10, Jer 8:20, 34:17, Eze 9:4, 14:17, 37:1, 39:15, Isa 43:2, Joe 3:17, Nah 1:15

In a Whisper of Time

The old woman's heart still broken by angry lovers reaches out for intimacy- will you hold me? man wants to reach out, wants to hold, wants ... torn by his mortality and the consuming age of the old woman he touches her body sifting through the earth of her crooked fingers seeking softness like violets pushing through rocks and sand, who can hold a stone close to their hearts and not be moved? only someone who has not lost everything? she covers the graves and the remains with the earth that moves through her and touches what's immoveable and shifts the things that need to be displaced, then he reaches out to hold her dark eyes, her broken hair, the threads, the bones by which he is reminded of how he treated all the fair and lovely things of earth, the old woman sighs from a memory, which seemed like yesterday, of a love when everything was new, in a whisper of time, in a fold in the unfolding universe, and the spirit went out.

2005.05.10

The Pen

The pen
is mightier
than the sword
the spirit more so
than the pen.
The Holy Spirit
above all else
indwells in word
and man.

We write the thoughts
we feel
to open the door
of the heart.
A breeze flows through
and alerts us to
a world that lies
apart.

A world
that when
the Creator began
encompassed
the Word, the Spirit
and man.

2005.05

The Desert Manna

I only took what's mine
but I had had enough
for all my members.
"What is it"?[5]
you say,
there was sufficient
for each day
involved as I was
in the things of the world

I searched for destiny
and did not realize
it was bound up
in the sheaves of my life
My heart ached
for fulfillment
because now
was not enough —
I didn't want to be
too specific.

                                                       2005.06.4

Montmorency Falls

It was at Montmorency Falls
water coming down hard
scenes of yesteryear
my own, and Wolfe
had staged an encampment
felt like two cents, maybe more

---

[5] Manna: מָן literally, "what is it" Ex 16:15.

Then I saw the circle
shining round and bright
covenant of mercy
testament of light

He would not forsake me
let me know His hand
would counsel and console
from out the bitter land

I couldn't help but wonder
in all of this a plan
in the midst of spray and thunder
the sheep are guided in

I stepped inside the orbit
on the hard and ragged rock
some grass and purple flowers
thrived in the heavy damp

I let the sun enclose me
it ringed me with its fire
it satisfied a longing
and bid me not to tire.

                                            2005.08

2006

The Hidden Battle

Just after four a.m.
And just before springtime
Poor him!

If you don't do it, *hostie!*
who will?
Words need to be dropped like... well
only one need suffice
It's time
put on your most frail garments
buckle your scabbard
in your finest hour
The sword was unsheathed
and the battle called
while you reclined.
How could you know
that the silken web's weave
stretched while you slept
would lead to this?
It knitted its way
just on the border
of consciousness
The blade cut
the shame we hid behind
There is no recourse
to rationality
it will only work
if two or more or four
are committed to agree
Nothing like a national
works program

of Herculean scope
because it was more
like an afterthought
after you stopped – thinking
Just stop
It's enough to engage
and the spiders will work
on the details
The sceptre was thrown
it lay about
to all appearances
a broken branch
It was accidentally picked up
by the squeegee guy
who didn't know what he had
when he held it
because we all had to stop
at the crossroads
and wipe our eyes
and he would go to his grate
and be comforted
The sword remained unsheathed
I tried to put it behind me
but couldn't escape
the blood on the floor
it's now forever
everyone thing is compelled
to pull together
or rip apart
if we . . .

                                               2006.02.15

What? Evolution!

What? Does not fruit fly
in the face of an evolutionary tale
to what end expend
the sweet express avail

What hidden genetics germinate
hang out the dew to draw
some alien species unwittingly
takes of its best to replicate

What hope is there to be?
life hangs by threads on trees
what purpose generated
an apple consummated

What could an inanimate know
that loss of life would sow
either by ground or bee
its own immediacy

To what end expend again
on what continuity depend
life determined by the unknown
the arbour by itself is sown?

Life taken up by the swarm
a species yet unborn
life released from the hold
life's decease yet unfolds

Things determined
rationally
neglect the mystery
of the unconditionally free.

                                        2006.08.21

The Deranged Birds

The deranged birds
tore through the heart
of the downtown
They tore through the heart
of every man, woman, and child
spilling human blood liberally
many of us felt an affinity

They were led by misbelief
to kill men, women, and children
some sought to pardon them
because they were only human
but they left their humanity behind
when they took up arms
against everyone
and lost perspective

They felt a mission from their system
to challenge everyone
to their own belief
a mania of spiritual purity
like a rabid ethnicity
running with frozen rage
to appease a consuming god

Their hatred was wreathed in smiles
their death was wreathed
by a maniacal misunderstanding
of life's purposeful dissolution
the entity had
little tolerance for human frailties

How do we respond to nothing
except to be very quiet
let no word disturb
the passing wind
created by vacuousness
be still and witness
the rush to violence.

                                                          2006.09.13

Wendy

On the occasion of her
61st birthday,
September 4, 2006
This weekend at the
Botanical Gardens
Wendy crawled through the
10-inch gap under
the iron fence so I
wouldn't have to walk around
with my bad knee to get the car
This is typical of Wendy
let me tell you all about her

At twenty she and her friend Michael
hitchhiked the U.S. with her cat
Pistol
hopping semis and sleeping in the cab
got to Frisco had an alien encounter
after Michael prophesied
life on other worlds
(confirmed by headlines)
Hung out in Gardner Colorado
living in adobes
checking out the scenery
standing on a rattler
(sent her screaming)
Prior to this she danced in France
avec Les Feux Follets
(The Fou Follets
as Sullivan called them)
she danced for him
and also in North Bay
and parts of the U.S.
that's all she wanted was

to dance
but she got stuck in London
by romance.
You'd think she's working
with people in crisis
she's an empath
it's only natural
Her life is weird (like mine)
that's why we're together
She loves our son – Jasper
I called him Jasper Gates
from the Bible not literal
She'd do anything for him
like drive to Disney World
in the Renault 5 – while
I stayed in Rigaud
She killed a big ugly spider
with the Bible she was reading
to them – Jasper and his buddy
"Hey mom! There's a spider"
and "wham" on the tent wall
it splat real flat
then Jasper had to drive
used the starter motor
crossed the field and got them
avoiding water moccasins
I couldn't imagine what
the heck was happening
Called to say that
she was stuck in third
(the engine block had fallen
on the gear shift lever)
took her mom to Dundee
When mom was eighty
toured the highlands
going down the wrong side

hoped she wouldn't hit them
she's a bit dyslexic
Found Cupar Abbey
a plaque on a boulder
her mom's maiden name
paid their respects to MacDonald
(laid low at Glencoe)
and the big Mother at Balmoral
She felt young again 'cause
her heart was in the highlands
She liked to hang with drummers
when she was younger
and once with el Cohen
it was an endless summer
hung out with Sidetrack,
jazz bands and the like
her dad built airplanes
mom sold real state
Jasper is a D.J.
she's my love
mais où est ma femme gitane ce soir?

2006.09.21
Figure 1: Wendy

The Absolute

The absolute hung by a thread
relative to what was said
The thread grew even finer still
until it only hung by will

When will had long since passed its time
and nothing else would hold the line
Then faith was born from aught
when absolute was brought to naught.

2006.10.16

The Crows

Ah Nature! Throw open the window
to see the trees sway, the branches play
against the windowpane
and here and there
I could learn to pick out
the sounds of cardinals
sparrows, robins and ...
but what the hell is that cacophony
at first a distant moan
crescendoing to a very distinct
punctuated cawing of crows?
What is so important
that a hundred throats complain?
A disastrous board meeting
or has the market gone insane?
This reeks of that old complaint
how long has it been going on?
The crows refrain
no time for god
no moment of peace
no release, there's business

that needs attending, as professionals
we propose
forbid we acquiesce and trust our lives
to the mercy of the infinite
It would be too subservient
(as public servants)
to wait awhile
and give an ear to
what's most worthwhile

I'll slam the bloody window
give it an hour
maybe they'll take their meeting
someplace else.

                                                          2006.10.26

2008

Green Olive Tree

The oil was expressed to the last drop
and Tree stood parched and bare
her leaves had sheltered generations
who now were beyond her care

The vegetation was uprooted and burned
when the Roman roads cut through
yet Olive had clung to the side of the slope
for the sake of friends she once knew

Her fingers tore through the limestone bed
to squeeze every drop from the ground
she was keeping alive a memory
when Father's tears touched her gown

There was also – in the long distant past
her sister Terebinth told
three humans – indescribable
who sheltered under her fold

They appeared in an instant as if through a door
and suppered on wheat cakes on the soft desert
    floor
while the lady could be heard
laughing softly to herself in the distance

In another instance but difficult to place
when late an elusive soul
had turned up the soil at Olive's feet
and buried shards of an alabaster bowl

She remembered it well as a time out of time
being so perpetually perpendicular
a rush of human emotions had overwhelmed
so beyond her she no longer could care

Then that Man came around
at least in essence a man
it seemed he had passed through Olive's Press
and poured out his blood on the sand

The blood carried the scent of Nard
made you want to turn inside out
mixed with an anguished beauty
night collapsed under Sick Man's rout

Later the Romans salted the ground
which made for a very lean year
so she turned on her back away from the blast
and stretched leaves toward her distant-most care

She was waiting for the Man to come back again
but felt she would probably die in the interim.[6]

2008.01.31
(Gen 18, Psa 52:8, Jer 11:16, Mat. 26:36, Rom 11:17)

---

[6] Originally published in *The Tree of Life*, Wipf and Stock, 2021.

A Note from the Future

Hi! – To whom this note is received
I've just found out that the lease
on my cryogenic container
is about to terminate and
I would like to make it
perfectly clear my
condition will
T E R M I N A T E
(I hope to convey the
seriousness of my situation)
Although I had managed
to accumulate a substantial sum
in the short term: 1950 – 2008 CE
I hope you can appreciate that I fell
just short of the mark on the
hundred-year contract
which would have provided for
a complete resuscitation as well as
a total reconstruction
and would have
allowed me a fully renewed
virile, strong Max-Life Body
(You can imagine my excitement)
I will only require a paltry $99k
to carry me over to the resurrection
period. And you will be amply rewarded for
your desperately needed generosity
in the near term

I guarantee on my departed word
to release hitherto unknown funds
from very secure investments
of which I am the sole party
to said knowledge

Please, please, get back to:
my ambivalent dimension
(Which is neither here nor there)
via petersgate at universal dot he
and refer to ID: ruahuman2.

                              2108 – 2008.04.14

On Mount Sinai's Tortured Height

Fire, fire, burning bright
on Mount Sinai's tortured height
what immortal hand or eye
engraved the fearful scratch inscribed?

On what mountain, on what plain
did the Holy Ghost proclaim?
by whose darkened heart received
by what diamond quill conceived?

What the spirit, what the man
who stood to hear the Maker's plan?
What the anguish in his bones
by what deep did he atone?

By what letter, by which word
did the furnaced wrath ensure?
by what boundless intelligence
did the law transfigure man?

When the tribes threw down their spears
and watered idols with their tears
did He rage his work to see?
did He who made the lamb believe?

2008.06.15

The Five Talents

Dear God, hello
I feel I have wasted
much of my life on
useless things, sometimes
and many times, even, my
involvement with people is
not helpful or even profitable
if relationships can be evaluated
by currency. At one point,
for example, you gave me
five talents.
Of which I apportioned them
five ways, knowing
full well that investments
are libel to failure. If I can recall
one was to finance, of which one went to
Nortel (and others) failed
abysmally. One was to repay debt
which was an unfortunate plague
on my life. And another talent went
for personal satisfaction. Of the five
of which I can account for four,
only the one which went to bless

others, may unbeknownst to me prove
profitable. Part of which secured the passage
of Three (headline them please)
Russian Jews to Israel.
I trust they're doing well
at my expense – at least it was You who
would ultimately provide. So my dismal
experience in world finance
and the sum total of the five talents
rests on the shoulders of the Three
Russian Jews. I only hope that
three out of five, will help me survive
that is, I'm counting on Your grace
not to judge me too harshly
in the things of the world
and that for any future investments
(if I could have Your attention
for another minute) I or You
that is, We, would be more successful
my wife is depending on it.

2008.06.25

Interchangeable Nature

Waves lapping at the shore
beg for more
waves lapping at the shore
waves lapping at the shore
beg for more
waves lapping at the shore

eyes laughing ashore
beg for more
eyes laughing ashore eye

the waves lapping at the shore
begging for more
eyes laughing ashore

waves laughing assure
waves laughing
waves lapping at the shore
beg for more
waves laugh at
the man who waves laughing

He waves the laugh
manning the waves
to shore the man
to wave ashore the lapping
and beg for more

Waves to man the shore
volunteers to man the waves
shores to wave the man
alms to heave the waves
to wave the man ashore.

        Maine, 2008.07.23

The Acacia Box

In the heat of the day
the Acacia box sweated
Gum Arabica
and gold fumes
ions vaporized by the intensity
of the supernormal
electric discharge
of all things returning
in an instant
to source
The occasional drops
of human sweat
splattered and sizzled
leaving a faint dusting
of salt particles
on the two-winged beings
riding shoulder high
on the heaving
Earth-Bound Box Bearers
swaying to the rolling hills
lumbering side-saddle
half conscious of the un-matter
Ancestral Proton Box
devised in the primordial thought
of the Who Am.
The Box preserved the loci
of commemorative
intersecting inter-times
supernormal times
when the Who Am and the Earth-Bounds
had connected
Meanwhile the earth bodies
were barely conscious of
the immaterial source

that made their hearts beat.
In another life
a similar box had housed
pairs of kinds and kings
and human remains
but today it contained
desert provisions
a stick, and some writings
for the long haul
which would have lifted
the lowest spirits.
Around sundown
the box would jerk to a halt
it was like carrying around
a mini universe
you didn't want to be too close
to the reactor core
in case someone
inadvertently
short-circuited the whole thing.
Of course it was only a box
but again someone
had inadvertently
and it was like
throwing the switch
on the whole universe
and I'm telling you
it was lights out
for a split–eternity
I didn't want to mess with it
When it was properly positioned
there was a shreening type of sound
like two dimensions caressing
and the cold fire light
sort of arched between the two-winged beings
I can't say it was unearthly

it was actually fundamentally
more essentially material
than the vaporous ground
we thought we stood on.
And again
you didn't want to be too close
but it had a human quality,
I mean in so far as humans
you couldn't really compare
the essence and quality of emotion,
a profound sweetness
of honey and coriander
the immeasurable vastness
of its particularity and identifiably unique
singularly touchingly personal
put the finger on
what you were feeling
You couldn't ask for anything
every question was met
with the most immediate and profound
basic life substance.
Caught as we all were with our grievances
we were compelled
to relinquish any earthly reason
for our condition
because the sum of us
was bound up in the box
and the aggravations
melted
because the most essential
that is the nucleus
of the acacia tree frame
with the metallic overlay
ultimately reordered
whatever fragmentary dissociative
cast on the rubble heap

of life-crisis criticality,
that is, life mattered
and nothing mattered
and every frigging problem
had a resolution of sorts
So, it was like
teleport till sunup
and would you have thought you had slept?
Nope!
But there we were
ready to roll
that was us,
the heaving
Earth-Bound Box Bearers
swaying to the rolling hills
lumbering side-saddle,
half conscious of the un-matter
Ancestral Proton Box.

2008.10.22

Word Construction

Sometimes words
come in rhymes
people relate
thoughts aligned

Sometimes words
come in threes
that's odd they say
I'm not too pleased

Sometimes words
fall out of the sky
feelings collapse
the world's awry

Sometimes words
come in tens
there could be a percent
from the publishing men

Sometimes words
are out of place
and the metre and thoughts
suffer their state.

2008.10.26

The Native American Woman

The Native American Woman
was in the news
she had had a long history
of religious abuse

The North American Church
was in the news
she had a long history
of religious abuse

So, what happened to
the poor, mournful and meek
seekers after righteousness
the merciful, pure and peace?

I think there is a relationship
from the very first
when we broke ties
with the Hebrew church

We cut off our feet
to spite the earth
and laid our heads
on Grecian verse

This Native Woman said
It's very clear
despite all the abuse
her words are pure

"One foot in the grass
One foot on the sidewalk
This is Jesus
and this is the Church"

"The softness of the grass
The hardness of the Church
It has not been kind to our people
historically"[7]

---

[7] Mary Fontaine, Westminster Presbytery B.C. Canada, quoting an unidentified Native woman on aboriginal redress. Listen Up: Global TV

And there you have it
her words are plain
we've forced the via Latina
on the Aboriginal claim.

       2008.10.26

I Want to Take Refuge in Earth

I will hide in grandmother Nature
I'll become the bark on the oak
or the green needles that cloak
and are softly, softly gathered
around the evergreen pine

that's where I'll hide
in plain view, an honorary elm
in the town square without a hint of care
for those who feel – au contraire

I'll bend on the bough of the willow
by the rushing rivulet
and maybe for once
march with the majestic Ents
against evil Mordor
then cautiously retreat through the underbrush
with the little folk to their rooted abode
where I'll dine, underground
on elderberry wine, spruce tea
and taste the black earth
where there is no sound
except my heart
assuring me that life
is better spent in slower growth

I will polish the roots of the maple
that embrace my black hole
I will clean their limbs
totally impractical
to anyone but me
and if someone says
Tree! Give up the person you are hiding
I will respond
I am no longer me
there is no hiding – what you see is a tree

A tree tea have I negotiated
and made peace with arbour society
my humanity has transcended dexterity
and now I am earthbound
and although apparently immobile
we hold hands underground
praying for deliverance from violence

Our leaves cry out for comfort
we can't handle the theological tension
So, I want to thank you God
for preparing the garden bed
I can choose whichever species
to hide my human head
and if you perceive a Tree
that appears oddly human instead
approach with gentleness please
and query with a passionate – squeeze.

2008.12.27

2009

The Tree

Let me speak plainly
as a tree
I am not so normally
communicative
as you've perceived

I would like to think ...
but by then
so many things would have happened
what can I say
the thought was in transition

I was going to make a statement
something precise
the idea had potential
I think you would have liked ...
and would have been happy with ...

As usual we are very separate
you and I
I'm hoping you're getting the sense
it's not that I haven't tried
I thought I was specific

My word was on the verge of ...
I was so very proud
and swelled with expectation
but could plainly see – your look of
I think you've realized my consternation

I had to let the idea fall
there was a problem
and as you mentioned
it died on the vine
I don't think the failure was my limitation

And you know!
the paper you're holding – is me!
Shouldn't I get a little credit?
how far do I have to go, as a tree . . .?

Well, I've said what I said
you can see you've consistently expected more
than what was given
and there was only the one word
which was so very obviously . . .

I hope you will take it seriously
I've gone to great lengths
trying to extricate myself
from my communication

And I just remembered
of course you'll remember
what this is all about
I am only trying to say
I am happy to be
of service.

                                          2009.01.10

The Train Station

The train station
may be only a train station
but we are strangely transplanted
very conscious that
our roots are showing
the organism takes out leaf and quill
to prescribe symbols for progress
but even that process
is a terrible revelation
as if the machine would shudder
in an act of self-revelation
spitting out vegetable matter
churning its gears
the organism is frozen
to the waiting room chair.

            2009.01.11

I Swallowed the Bitter Pill

I swallowed the bitter pill
and accepted the profound covenant
with the fact
that I had to get by
with the way it is
nothing I could do
would make a difference
and I betrayed you to
the onerous reality
of the way it was
the fire went out
I didn't even know
it had been lit.

            2009.06

2011

Jasper

I dreamed of a branch
there was something
out of the ordinary
the more I fixed my look
a stub on the branch
reacted
in anxious anticipation
it felt revealed
I might not have known
but it upped and ran away
a small elfin forest creature
a son to be
born only that day

Accompanied by the strains
of RVW's *Lark Ascending*
on the BBC in the wee hours at 6180 KHz

A premonition of that gentle elf
that cheerful cherub
with the milkweed hair
you were always a compassionate soul
you wiped my boots with the towel
after I dragged my body home
selling cookbooks in the rain.
You poured out your entire savings
of nickels, pennies, and dimes
for the Witnesses' who came beseeching
you were distraught
by the condition of the Ethiopians
and begged us to support them

you loved your dog Arana
which you named after the sign (Arena)
you thought it was a good name

You looked like Winston C.
sometime before the Boers
and possibly after WWIII.
You are still a soul of compassion
always thinking about others
which has gotten you into
some real disasters.
It must be difficult
for an elfin forest creature
to live in the downtown
in the heart of the downtown
with all the other forest creatures
ragged and unruly
ranging wild in their grunge pits
locking horns and bodies
in their furry underworld
and you love to engage
the fiery heartbeat
as it swarms the barroom floor.

I could never engage
the tempestuous herd
like you.
All the best in your quest
Jasper
I wish you a place
where elfin beings
and other mythical creatures
rest in the beginnings
of creation.

> Dad
> Dream, 1977.10.21
> Poem, 2011.12.29
> Figure 2: The milkweed hair

2012

The Three Types of Fusion Process

In Varennes Quebec
at the Tokamak de Varennes
Hydro Quebec
managed to sustain
the fusion process
for several milliseconds
that was a big accomplishment
considering it took
many megawatts to produce
a fraction of a second of
measurable power
The mechanism consists
of magneto-plasma-toroids
vessels for nuclear containment
and these are housed in
a large black cube
similar to the Kaaba in Mecca
or the monolith in 2001
so there might be a relationship there

Several millennial ago
when there were many swords
in the land and people were
indiscriminately hung up
or cut down
a man was born in a cattle stall
next to the House of Bread
he also initiated
a fusion process

which has sustained itself
for what appears to be an indefinite period
using the principle
of loving your enemy
he delegated twelve humans
most of whom were killed
but the principle survived
he identified
the magneto-plasma process
as loving God first
loving your neighbour
and doing your best to love those
who were doing their best
to hate you
it seems to be working
since there are still many individuals
living by that principle
but it's not easy – when you're on
the hot seat

Also, on a more common note
the male and female ($\male + \female = !$)
of the species
have been using the same principle
of loving each other
which also creates
a sustainable fusion.

2012.03.26

A Fine Mist in the Night

A fine mist
hangs
not quite fallen
down
a swirl of rain
winds
its way around
it doesn't care to land
why would it
it moves
with the tide of the air
it floats
flittering faint
around the tops of
trees
no gravity
keeps it
there suspended
on the wide tide
of the air highway
wide tide of air
whispering
to the night
the night
the night
the night
while whispering softly
to the earth's ear
ear earth
ear earth
ear earth
earth ear
lofty am I
loftily I'll fly foolishly

foolishly
it patters my lips
in the damp.

                                                            2012.05.1

The Cardinal's Message

I was alone
I thought I was alone
a bird in the tree
spoke solemnly
twee twit twit
of course
it was in the style of Morse
it said

twit twit twit twit
twit twit
hi it said
hi it said

twit twit
twit twit twit
twit twit

is I
is I
I his.

                                                           2012.05.1

2013

Two Mating Dragonflies

Two mating dragonflies
catapulting through the skies
perpetuating baby lives
by the sea

Four wings are one
not to be undone
their passion in the sun
feeling free

Can't hope to match their bliss
sex in the air abyss
what a way to kiss
consummated wilderness.

                                            Maine, 2013.07.31

2014

The Mystical Messianic Turns of the Wheel

Remember Chinese Gordon[8]
he was a singular man
he fought in the Crimea[9]
(The Charge of the Light Brigade)[10]
and in Chinese lands
in the Opium Wars[11]
a blight on British commerce?

Later
with the blessing of Britain
And the Qing Dynasty
He came against
Hong Xiuquan[12]
a "Heavenly King"
and "brother of Christ"
during the Taiping Rebellion
a forerunner of Chinese Nationalism.
It must have been odd
for the Christian Gordon
to come against "Jesus' brother"
but he prevailed

---

[8] Major-General Charles George Gordon, CB (28 January 1833 – 26 January 1885)
[9] October 1853 – February 1856
[10] Alfred, Lord Tennyson; 1809-1892
[11] 1839-1860
[12] Hong Xiuquan (1 January 1814 – 1 June 1864)

In 1883
Gordon
found "Gordon's Calvary"
at the Place of the Skull
600 meters north of
(and an alternative to)
the Holy Sepulchre in Jerusalem

He had governed the Sudan
under the auspices of the viceroy of Egypt
Raghib Pasha[13]
suppressing revolts and
thwarting the slave trade
which caused havoc
to the commerce
of the region

Eventually
he was recalled to
extricate British nationals, which he did

Into the Mahdi's camp
rode Gordon and guide
unarmed and intent
to settle the divide
astounded the rebels
did not react
for Gordon forever
was a man of tact [14]

---

[13] Isma'il ibn Ahmad ibn Hassan bani Yani (1819–1884), Prime Minister of Egypt in 1882
[14] Khartoum (1966) Charlton Heston, Laurence Olivier

In the final exchange
with the Mahdi
Muhammad Ahmad[15]
(the Muslim messiah)[16]
Gordon was killed.

In 1885
Gratton Guinness[17]
deciphered the numbers in Daniel
to prophesy the liberation
of Jerusalem – in 1917
which Allenby[18] accomplished

The Arab prophesied
that Jerusalem would ne'er fall
until the Nile waters
came up to the wall
this Allenby obliged
in his unwitting style
no oil through the line
but water from the Nile

Remember
Amin el-Husseini[19]
many would prefer to forget
the grand mufti of Jerusalem
allied with Hitler

---

[15] Muhammad Ahmad bin Abd Allah (August 12, 1845 – June 22, 1885)
[16] http://en.wikipedia.org/wiki/List_of_Mahdi_claimants
[17] Henry Grattan Guinness D. D. (11 August 1835 – 21 June 1910)
[18] Field Marshal Edmund Henry Hynman Allenby, GCB, GCMG, GCVO (23 April 1861 – 14 May 1936)
[19] Haj Mohammed Effendi Amin el-Husseini (c. 1897 – 4 July 1974)

and called for the extermination of the Jews
He was wanted
by the Allied War Crimes Commission
but was sequestered
in the Levant.
He had suggested to Himmler
that the Nazis
were not doing enough
to kill the Jews[20]

The religious Husseini
managed to abort
and confounded obstructed
the most innocent accord
whenever an Arab
would try to make peace
he was sure to end up
by the mufti deceased

Orde Wingate[21]
went, where no one had gone before
he trained up the early remnants
of the IDF

Remember
Abdullah of Jordan[22]
he and his brother Faisal[23]

---

[20] Bartley Crum; Behind the Silken Curtain (Simon and Shuster 1947) p.111

[21] Major General Orde Charles Wingate, DSO & Two Bars (26 February 1903 – 24 March 1944)

[22] Abdullah I bin al-Hussein, King of Jordan (February 1882 – 20 July 1951) born in Mecca, assassinated in Jerusalem. Ruler of Transjordan and Jordan from 1921 to 1951

[23] Faisal bin Hussein bin Ali al-Hashimi, (20 May 1885 – 8 September 1933). King of the Arab Kingdom of Syria in 1920,

allied with Lawrence (of Arabie)
for the Arab liberation

Faisal and Weizmann
concluded the
Faisal–Weizmann Agreement[24]
hoping for peace between
Arab and Jew

King Hussein and King Faisal
together they rode
to navigate the dreams
of the Hashemite hoard
The one he was killed
by the muftis' long arm
and Faisal was poisoned
To ensure Arab decorum

Rafik Hariri[25]
Prime Minister of Lebanon
he encountered a similar fate
killed by the Party of God [26] [27]

On January 6th, 1982 at 2 p.m.
Ron Wyatt discovered
the Ark of the Covenant

---

and King of Iraq from 23 August 1921 to 1933. A member of the Hashemite dynasty

[24] Faisal–Weizmann Agreement, 3 January 1919

[25] Rafic Baha El Deen Al Hariri (1 November 1944 – 14 February 2005) Prime Minister of Lebanon

[26] Hezbollah Wikipedia accessed March 2024

[27] CBC Investigation: Who killed Lebanon's Rafik Hariri? By Neil Macdonald, CBC News Posted: Nov 21, 2010:
http://www.cbc.ca/news/world/cbc-investigation-who-killed-lebanon-s-rafik-hariri-1.874820

Remember Nguyen Chi Thien [28]
Vietnamese dissident
history professor and poet
taught that the US and not Russia
had conquered Japan in WWII
for which he was incarcerated
without a pencil, he managed
to etch his 700 poems, into his brain

Today
the local Mahdi
cuts my hair fine and quick
he doesn't charge
an arm and a leg.

                              2014.02.14

---

[28] Nguyen Chi Thien, 27 February 1939 – 2 October 2012

Principles

It's been a while
although it seems
like just another
a horrible dream
in June a hundred
Princip shot Franz
out in the open
I can't get over
the social was broken
the hole gapped wide
they had to act
he had his reasons
they had theirs
what was he thinking?
millions will die
he lit the match
for the conflagration
you think it'll help
it doesn't solve
they've got one view
others have theirs.

2014.02.28

Cpl. Cirillo

The shepherds wait by the fence
their boundaries exploded
a thousand-fold
since last they saw him
the master unfurled to the wind
he was here with the plates
now he is there
in the step, in the leaves, in the look
the look as fathomless

as the breeze
that carried the smell
of his boots
the scent of belonging
that even now is
a mist on the morn
the dew on the blade
Gone in the heat of madness
the son will be glad to remember
the life tied to the shepherds
transient images tied
to the life of a dog, the life of a man
Heartfelt.

                              Killed 2014.10.22
                            Written 2014.10.29

On the Plaines

James and Louis-Joseph
are seated on the Plaines
mindful of the game
of chess being played, out
along the fallen tree
They eyed the broad horizon

Time narrowed
the waters Narrowed
in a quarter hour
the fates conspired
the shot decided

They played their piece by royal decree
"The boast of heraldry, the pomp of pow'r,
And all that beauty, all that wealth e'er gave,
Awaits alike th' inevitable hour.
The paths of glory lead but to the grave."

The pieces congregated
in formal liturgy
a dance of anticipation
of ancient pedigrees.

2015

As Time Goes By

In the evening
at 7 p.m.
Brian would call
to tell me when
As Time Goes By
came on again.
He never failed
to alert me to
he said it was
'his' program
I said it was 'mine' too

We sat in separate
rooms apart
he with his collection
of video art
me with my books
and tea, and wine
we lived our
collective lives
sublime.

                                                   2015

The Magnificent Chariot

The grail of our circumlocution
The cup we bought
was delicately wrought
in sea glass pearl
it held our
expectations
our dreams
the romance
of the unforeseen
to glide
without attendant means
it was a beginning
until we graduated

It evolved
(if colours evolve)
into an earthenware jar
into a bronze haze hue
possessing
energy indescribable
managed by millions of hands
handshake after handshake
turning, twisting, warning, signaling
accelerating, regenerating, circumventing,
navigating, almost beyond our control
communicating, talking back
(a little neurotic)
if I died
it would send miserable condolences
to the nearest constabulary.

2015.05.1

By Way of the Land Laid Waste

Whither to the wasteland comes
the sacred cup
the world undone
guided by hearts ablaze
what to make
of the dreadful maze
only to set sight
on an unearthly vector

What can passion have to do
within the confines
where the waters move
spiraling ever downward
except to steer
by that unseen star
guided by faith and fate
to Avalon's bar

All we are left
with a ruddy cup
a distant image
of the Saviour's last sup
clinging to scant hope
from endless strife
the other worldly intrudes
within our earthen life.[29]

            2015.09.30

---

[29] Originally published in *The Tree of Life*, Wipf and Stock, 2021.

2016

Memorial for Stan

I planted a butternut
in my parent's garden.
much later my father called
"Do you mind if I cut it down?
the acid's destroying the vegetables"
of course, dad
the vegetables
are more important

later
I bought a tree for my parents
from a man who rode motorcycles
and arm wrestled
and had a nursery
in Copemesh, Michigan
he grafted ancient species
redwoods, sequoia, willow and oak
and preserved their lineage.
"All memory is trapped in DNA
epigenetically," a parent-ly

He said he had been ordered
by an archangel
after he died and revived
I believed him, totally
He gave me his cell
He had fond memories of Montreal
I never called

Genesis says
we're taken from the ground
for carbon, we are
and carbon we shall return
or something similar

I hope my parents
memory will be
somehow sequestered
in a tree
as well as the hearts and minds
of those that loved them.
                                        2016.02.22

Eldercare Entertainment at the Speed of Light

I was watching the TV
in the room
in the dark
with the TV turned off
It was entertaining
that's why people watch
TV. I could have watched the wall
but that would be strange
and harder to explain
and the TV entertained.
The lilac leaves danced
on the screen
reflected by the
streetlamp in the dark.
back and forth
back and forth
lovely.
It was easier to watch the screen

than stare at the glare
of the streetlamp
which was muted by the screens
reflection
in the dark
not so harsh
as the streetlamp
on the outside
Inside
hundreds of tiny colored windows
refracted by the outside light
on the screen
red, blue, green
red, blue, green
Nice. Colorful. Entertaining.
Like the apartment block
beside the outside lamp
with the people
behind the windows
behind the shades
behind their sunglasses
in front of their TV
It occurred, to me
that the TV had bared its soul
what I thought was out was in
the colored windows
of the TV looking, at me
which I could see
the colours of its eyes
the pixilated
red, blue, green rods
staring blank faced
at me. Hundreds of tiny windows
magnified a hundred-fold
looking.
Trying to understand

why I was looking
at it.
You can learn a lot
from watching TV
in the dark
in the room
with your mind
turned off.

>   2016.05.09 03:00
>   The day after Mother's Day

Narrative in Transition

I was born
near L'Oratoire Saint-Joseph
on the rue Frère André
back when it was called Coronet
in St. Mary's Hospital
not too far

The Queen she toured
in '51, down St. Mary's Road
(I was on the balcon)
had she made peace
with the cousin Catholique
for heaven's sake

I collected rocks
and dreamed, absentmindedly
and wrote poems
and was accused
of plagiarism, at twelve
a simple poem about Santa Claus, that rhymed

I drifted into the Navy
and quickly drifted out

(the absent minded are not meant for battle)
I wrote, and wrote, poems
of anguished love, naked ladies
and read the dictionary (very revealing)

Dr. Cathleen Going
taught me theology in '63
she was kind-hearted
and gave me a thirty (percent)
I would occasionally correspond
she used to be the abbess at Farmington Hills

In time, I got caught up
in spiritual things
and alien beings
yet all the while
I studied assiduously
hoping to connect, the thoughts I had collected

When I got really down
I'd listen to Johnny Cash
In the Holy Land
singing, *He Turned the Water into Wine*
we went to the same school of theology, virtually

Eventually
I was awarded a degree
I exceeded where no one had gone before
taking a mere thirty, years to complete

Not to appear totally, vacuous
I did try to build
a flying bicycle
and other sensible things

I was commended in La Presse
for my sculpture
(Russian constructivism)
and built a pyramid
that dried tomatoes
(without having to go to Egypt)

In July of '68
the Virgin Mary appeared
to the St. Jean family
a momentous occasion
I know cause
at the same instant
I separated from my body

In '84 I got a brand new
secondhand car, license # CHP
I searched the airwaves
for a radio station
later to find
WCHP in nearby Champlain
(I listened carefully) it was a sign from God

Gradually
my poetry returned
after being struck by lightning
by Lonergan's *Insight*
the tyranny of rationality

I eventually
extricated myself
from numerous
damnedly dogged dogmas
and am free to breathe
except for the intricacies of grammar
etiquette, diet, and politics

We try our best
to manage between
possibility and probability.

2016.05.27

My Love is like a Red Red Rose

My love is like a red, red rose
her scent a light to hearts aglow
she tends her garden wild and free
colored by violets and mulberry trees

She makes her space, sacred and still
lightened by the twitter of the cardinal
neighbours stop by, barely inclined
to notice an Eden, from time before time

She tends the hearts of those in need
they forget for a moment, the wounds that bleed
her words are simple, to the point
enough to redirect, lives out of joint

My love is like a red red rose
so soft her touch begets
my love is like a red red rose
the hills will not forget

She wanders through the vales dim
she rides the windy shore
her step is soft like veiled perfume
her dance will still the floor

My love is like a red red rose
that soothes the hardened heart
she will not heed the pointed thorn
that's meant to harm the lark

She whiles her way upon the sea
of life's humanity
she sees the charm in every man
and is quick to set them free.
                        For Wendy. Hurleys, 2016.06.22

2017

The Irish Rover

Last night
we were sitting
round the fire
by the starlight
we smoked some beer

we sang a coupla songs
just to shake
all the shit off
and the frigging blues

we were cold
and tired
so lonely
and so wired
we couldn't even bend
to tie our shoes

the night was real bitter
made you feel like a quitter
every dream you ever had
poured down the gutter
what the hell
what's to live for
when the whole world's
a shit hole
it couldn't get much worse
then when you lost your best friend
in the night

I was looking through the flames
coulda sworn I'd gone insane
a dude was sitting
where there's no one before

he was grinning
like a maverick
strumming that ole black magic
on his very beaten
one hundred string guitar

the flames were dancing round him
as he pounded the ground in
and he squinted and hollered at the stars
some coyotes gathered round
they stood awestruck at the sound
and couldn't seem to shake off
all their wonder

it was Jesus Christ almighty
come to party on a Friday
when the whole world thought
they's having fun

he was jumping and a pounding
at the river's edge
resounding
as the stones themselves
were torn and turned to powder

we were jumping and a wailing
and we couldn't help but feeling
like we were Shadrach and Abednego
all over

the night was almost done
and we'd put the blues to ground
when he got up
to bid us adieu

we were lying in the grass
he said "that was a blast"
and he got up for a parting of the ways

in the soft morning light
he chuckled in delight
and as he sauntered off
he whistled
The Irish Rover.

                                                2017.08.25

Figure 3: The Irish Rover S.M.

Clarity

What time
should we leave?
I asked the proprietor
11:12 he said
11:12, it kept going
'round my head
ok, why be so specific
he seemed a simple man
(uncomplicated to be p.c.)
couldn't you say
quarter-after or
11 – thereabouts
well, if you say so, 11:12
I didn't say it out loud.
It took awhile to register
talk about complicated
obviously, a simpler man than I
we left at 12.

                                Burlington VT, 2018.05

2019

Esquimalt

In the museum sat
the attendant in the chair
a part of the memories
as quiet as
a display
or a functionary
either / or
for me
a part of the past
below the waves
the symbols crested
and troughed
bowed
and boughed.
Alert
the sentries
took their place
in the line of time
I was disquieted
not to have held
more firmly
the line
those who had held
stern to the end
God bless you
friend
if I can call you
if I could call you
I would
call on your valour
to hold steady

aye, with an eye
on the pole star
and the time
with a grip on the wheel
and to stand aloft
and sound the alarm
or stand down.
I will carry the tune
there will be
merriment
to lighten the load
the mighty chord
and mighty song
stand fast and
hold ground
my friend
stand fast.

                                                  2019.10.29

2021

The Aftermath

After the war
the question–why?
stretched across the gulf
of meaninglessness

the particles of humanity
which
had quietly assembled
lay on the concrete floor

We're ok, we said
unaware of the void
which had
delineated the terms of meaning

What we thought
was togetherness
was only a shared relief
from hopelessness

Normally we planned
on going from a to b
now, we get along
with x, y, and z.

                                                 2021.06.6

All Hands on Deck

All hands on deck
protect, protect.
All hands on deck
protect, protect.
We'll help you out
what about, what about.
We'll help you out
what about, what about.
haul up the mainsail
haul up the mainsail
what the heck
what the heck
the sun is over the yardarm
the sun is over the yardarm
spill the beans
spill the beans
be quiet
be quiet
please be quiet.

> Stephen & Vienna, 2021.07

Bug Book

bugs
some bugs are fast
And I'm fast too
and some bugs are slow
some bugs like flowers
other bugs like other bugs
bugs eat things.

> Vienna, 2021.07

No Never I Be

Querium haliacum
hallusogens, hallohah
wonder what
wonder he about
all de same
all de same
going up
going down
all about town
weird ass shalom
Miriam sometime home
salamander in the slammer
all night long
round about
sometime at night
bwing, bwing, bwing
him along and sing
why not?
oh I see, I see
zimalar, zimalar
o so zimalar
zing wee down
ole Ken song
down by freedom way
it's all hearsay, so say
the wanderings
wandering this
wandering that
I say, slay the drag
isn't he a cobbler?
—oops, stop
"woke up, got outa bed"
dragged an onion
across my

oh onion
my onion
halibee, halibee
in distress
don't go down de ding dong
don't go down de ding dong line
much as I would like
de ding, dang, dong

Yes but
soupy sales
by the coconut tree
calling for mama's
partiality

shredding, shredding, shredding
so much paperwork
ding dong, ding dong
"If you don't pay your taxes"
you know – dis is da
Arch EMP
don't bodder me widda
technical calamities
I'm busy at work
doing
noddink
zanks a lot, zanks a lot, zo long

So now I be wondering why
you be reading
dumb nonsense
maybe, stuck in turmoil?

"Ours not to reason why
ours but to do and…"
into the valley of debts
rode the six hundred.

2021.10.8

The Muse

My Lady
in the feeder
sipping sunflower seeds
kerchiefed and quaint
spoke silently
summoning words
out of birdsong
for me to recite.

2021.10.8

2022

Events in my Life Today

The refuse men
(a.k.a., waste collectors, garbagemen,
trashmen, binmen, and dustmen)
went, at a maddening pace
down the avenue
doing the 10k
they smoke
and occasionally
come up for air
Collecting black bags
which were heard all the while
crying out
refuse me not, refuse me not
flowers forgetting their roots
these are the refuse men
the refuseniks in training
for refusedom
these classes of society are closely allied to
a Dr. Yoshinori Ohsumi,
(a.k.a. 大隅 良典)
who established the principles
of autophagy
the parallels are striking
An hour later
the Bucher-Schörling Optifant
8000 street cleaner
collected
any miscellaneous droppings
a clean sweep

I omitted the most important event
Wendy, my wife, contacted Covid-19 today
April 20, 2022, a front-line worker
diligent, and always careful,
since the outbreak
it caused a
pulmonary embolism
I'm believing that
the principles of autophagy
the clean sweep, will help
they are also found in Matthew 17:21.[30]

                                                      2022.04.20

My Valentine

One heart, your heart
your love nourishes me
quietly, the strands of your being
the strands of your heart
silken threads of longing
unravel and wind
unwind and form
unsettle and caress
wordlessly, thoughtfully
without my knowing
plants growing in the night
our twisted limbs entwined
eerily reminiscent of ages long ago
you are mine
I am yours
my love.

                                                      2022.02.14

---

[30] The NU-Text omits this verse.

Cat Man Do

Cat man do
Cat man do
nobody knows
what the cat can do
blacker than ink wells
blacker than night
cat so black
so outta sight

So slinky black
so slinky light
this cat moves
like it don't seem right

Cat can do
Cat can do
outta the inside
into the no side
into the dark side
into the night

syncopated rhythm
syncopated time
this cat moves
between the rhyme

Cat man do
Cat man do
going to raise no
hullabaloo.

2022.08.03

Elizabeth

Elizabeth
carried the oxcart
with the common folk
through the separated Isles
isles of blessing from
the early Ages

She
drove
the battle-green truck
with the red mark of George
through the abyss
of desperation

Elisheva
swore
by the seven-fold
testament of the Most High
to be circumspect during
the frozen period

Elizabeth is
"some corner of a foreign field
that is forever" the Commonwealth
where her steps are traced
by the Middle folk
of the Shire

La mer, la mère, the mare
from sea to sea
her hand steady on the helm
her eye on the pole star, she navigated
from the river to the ends of the earth
ships of state

She honours
by the cross
those feet in ancient time that
walked upon the Island's mountains green
—nor did her sword sleep
in her hand.

2022.09.09

Gold Dust at My Feet

Through the window frame
of the door
the sun spills in
on the wooden floor

Grains of wood
laid bare
to the cool clean
autumn air

What once had been
the veins of trees
now they bear
human knees

Nearby a table
also basks
in the same warm light
from the same gold flask

On the table
on the plate
two sardines
to contemplate

Where once they played
in ocean deep
they now restore
my human need.

2022.11.9

Poem at Solstice

I am indivisible. Except by one. That is, i over 1, or i/1. In which case i am still i and am interchangeable with one. That is my relationship with u. Thankfully, we can agree at the intersection of i and u, where if u'll take the high road and i'll take the low road we can exchange without words. We are similarly composed as one, where we can b, in accord. The instant of intersection is an interval of eternity (since there is no place to go) or be displaced by place. Thank goodness for a sabbatical moment, like the Rest and Be Thankful on the A83 from Loch Lomond. A moment to encounter. All roads lead to, until there are no more, there's an apocalypse, back to square one. Mathematically, i = 1-2-b. Uniquely, the one gravitated out of nothing. How one is that? There was no other. A singular particle in an ocean on a universal wave in the matrix of chai.

2022.12.17

2023

Mourning Dove

Mourning dove
oh let it be
has thy love
forsaken thee?

Let no qualms
between thee come
nor let thy world
become undone

Whatever pictures
in the sky
have come to set
thy world awry

Leave these pictures
let them rest
they will find
their own bequest

For in thy beating
heart console
all that wonders
all that glows

Sanctify thy
weary name
always mournful
forever same

Comfort me
thy soulful song
comfort all
to God belong.

2023.09.06

Articles previously posted in The Montreal Review 2023 – 24

Let Us Make Man in Our Image - צלם, After Our Likeness – דמות (Gen 1:26)

The beginnings of the book of Genesis helps to situate man's place in creation, his essential nature, and his relationship to the divine. How do we identify with this incredible seemingly illusory statement that says that we embody the quality of our Creator? What is it, what is in us that somehow connects our being with the I AM. What is being, and what is ultimate Being in relationship. Not an easy task, but – a moment to appreciate.

Many of us have probably struggled with this verse, with our minds and hearts, trying to come to grips with the implications of its meaning. We are intelligent vessels of clay who occasionally have 'intimations of immortality.' Perhaps sometime in the hereafter we might have an occasion to realize what the verse truly means.

However, since we have been gifted with an intelligent mind, a heart, and an ability to come to an understanding, what is the process whereby we are able to communicate between our humanity and an infinitely indefinable Being. In other words, going from here and now, to everywhere all at once, all at the same time. A seemingly impossible venture. A task for artificial intelligence? Possibly. But we know that we are better than AI. Is a machine capable of love, of complete self-sacrifice for another? "A hireling, (the machine) he who is not the shepherd, one who does not own the sheep, sees the wolf coming and leaves the sheep and flees." (John 10:12)

The verse from Genesis also implies that we have a unique and very particular covenant with the creator. A covenant can be both general as well as specific. As in God's covenant to Abraham. "Look now toward heaven and count the stars if you are able to number them." And He said to him, "So shall your descendants be." (Gen 15:5 NKJV) Specifically each of us has a unique covenantal relationship to be realized which can deeply impact our personal well-being. We, in our moment, in our space, have the potential to experience the infinite.

It is always helpful to relate to someone's personal experience. I had that opportunity in the 60s when I was at the Ecole des Beaux Arts in Montreal. There I read Richard Maurice Bucke's, *Cosmic Consciousness* (E. P. Dutton 1901). Bucke was a trapper out west. In the winter of 1858, he was the sole survivor of a silver-mining party and had to walk out over the mountains and suffered extreme frostbite. As a result, his foot was amputated.[31] He returned to Canada, studied medicine at McGill, and became the superintendent of an asylum in London, Ontario. He was a friend and contemporary of Walt Whitman and shared many things in common with him. While in London, England he was reading some of the well-known poets with some friends in the 1870s. On the way home he experienced a "sudden conflagration in the great city," and next that "he himself was on fire." At this point he had a revelation. He "knew that the Cosmos is not dead matter but a living presence." (*Consciousness* p.8) His life is dramatized in the NFB film, *Beautiful Dreamers*, with Colm Feore (1990).

There are many other aspects to *cosmic consciousness* that are difficult to quantify in the scientific sense because of their particularity. They are unique and meaningful to the person concerned and

---

[31] Wikipedia. From: Bucke, Richard M. (June 1883). "Twenty-five years ago." Overland Monthly. I. (Second series) (6): 553–560.

possibly no one else. They are not replicable. There are many descriptors that define these experiences; serendipitous, synchronicity, non-local consciousness, a unique meeting of like minds. Some of these are defined in Carl Jung's "Synchronicity: An Acausal Connecting Principle." As well as by Dr. Stanley Krippner's work at the Maimonides Dream Laboratory in Brooklyn, NY. (*Dream Telepathy*, Macmillan, 1973). I met Dr. Krippner at a symposium at McGill titled: *Psychedelics and the Religious Experience*. It was held by Dr. Raymond Prince in the late 60s.

Several years ago, I created a workshop at the Thomas More Research Centre on non-local consciousness. https://thomasmore.qc.ca/thomas-more-research-centre . I related to the group my own somewhat simple experience in my twenties when I decided to hitchhike across Canada to find work in Edmonton. (I wanted to create a feeling with the group of the commonality of non-local consciousness). I told them that I had been apprehensive about the hitchhiking, and it was with good reason since I would be standing on a highway in the West Island for about eight hours before getting a lift. Before venturing out (in the late 60s), I decided to implement my newfound experience in TM meditation. While I was meditating, I realized that the experience of the here and now in meditation would be the same experience I would have if I meditated out west. So, the experience of distance, which was a cause for anxiety was mitigated by the feeling that the 'here and now' over here, would be the same feeling as the 'here and now' over there. The meditation inspired a sense of comfort within me. Others in the workshop were also able to connect to similarly meaningful experiences, which created a sense of unity.

Recently, I was talking to the local parish priest. We were talking about Padre Pio, the Italian mystic. He asked me "Do you know what bilocation is?" Yes, I said. The priest continued; Padre Pio in Italy would visit Cardinal Mindzenty in Hungary using bilocation. Mindzenty had been incarcerated and tortured by the communist government of Hungary (1949). This was an incredibly moving story. Padre Pio would 'visit' the cardinal in the Hungarian prison and bring him the blessed sacrament. These would be life sustaining moments for the cardinal since his status as a representative of the spiritual life of the Hungarian people was being mocked. He was dressed in a clown's outfit.[32] A prelude to the Ukraine? I had attended a service by Mindzenty at St. Joseph's Oratory in the 70s, so this story was more personally meaningful to me.[33]

If we consider the universe to be made of an entirely material state, then such things are impossible. But our notion of physics is changing. And again, these are unusually unique incidents. Will we deny all our eccentricities, especially our own? The point is that there can be a very unusually idiocentric element to the relationship between the human and the infinite. These experiences are valuable to the individual but may appear preposterous to an outsider. These are the moments when the infinite intrudes into the finite and gives further meaning to our lives.

I also had the opportunity to read portions of Bernard Lonergan's, S.J., *Insight, A study of human understanding.* (Longman's, Green, 1957, The Philosophical Library 1970). His analysis of cognitive operations helped me to organize my somewhat chaotic imaginings into a coherent understanding.

---

[32] Mindzenty, *Memoirs*, MacMillan, NY, 1974.
[33] Note: Mindzenty himself does not recount this experience in his Memoirs. I had to research it though accounts in the life of Padre Pio.

There is a pathway between the here and now and the realm of the infinite, or transcendent. From Lonergan's *operations*, I realized that there was a relationship between operations and being. There was an underlying symbolic form to consciousness which manifested itself in the Bible, and which facilitated a pathway, a cognitive link between our isolated sense as individual beings to our relationship with the divine. In other words, there is an element of intelligence intrinsic to being that has the capacity to relate to divine Being. I wrote about this understanding in *The Tree of Life, the form of human consciousness*:

(Wipf and Stock 2021). The major elements of the book can be previewed at: https://wipfandstock.com/9781725285545/the-tree-of-life/

On a more scientific level, there is the work of the HeartMath Institute developed by Doc Childre. Science shows that the brain has eighty-six billion neurons[34] compared to the heart which has 40,000. This was a very unusual development since it showed that the comparatively small heart brain was more essential to our welfare than our cerebral brain. The study by HMI showed that unless there was heart-brain coherence, unless the heart oversaw the brain, and not the brain in charge of the heart, there would be no coherence. The "heart sends more signals to the brain than the brain to the heart." (HMI) These studies were evaluated extensively using all electric data, as in EEG and ECG. In terms of the understanding that our being is made in the image of God, the study reveals the centrality

---

[34] Herculano-Houzel S (November 2009). "The human brain in numbers: a linearly scaled-up primate brain." Frontiers in Human Neuroscience. 3: 31. doi:10.3389/neuro.09.031.2009. PMC 2776484. PMID 19915731

of the heart as a conscious operator, as indicated by the many scriptural texts to which it is referenced.[35]

Science further developed the understanding of heart-rate variability. When HRV is flexible and responsive to its environment, it is a sign of health, compared to a very consistent and jagged rhythm, usually under stress, but which can also be a general condition. The Fascinating Relationship Between the Heart and Brain: HMI https://www.youtube.com/watch?v=WhxjXduD8q w&t=34s

There are many instances showing that the physical heart[36] embodies the consciousness of the deceased donor affecting the recipient of the transplanted heart. The most famous is the prosecution of a murderer of a young girl, based on the memory recall of the recipient, another young girl, induced by the donor heart memories.[37] These experiences are not meant to take away from the everyday reality that every heart has a very real conscious awareness, we are all capable of heart centered intuition. We are all able to identify that which we love, and the things and people that we are passionate about. But the experiences serve to dramatize the actual nature of heart consciousness.

HMI has also developed the Global Coherence Initiative at https://www.heartmath.org/gci which

---

[35] For reference: And God said to him (Abimelech) in a dream, "Yes, I know that you did this in the integrity of your heart." (Gen 20:6). For the word of God is quick, and powerful... a discerner of the thoughts and intents of the heart. (Heb 4:12) Blessed are the pure in heart: for they shall see God. (Mt 5:8) Jesus said unto him, thou shalt love the Lord thy God with all thy heart, and with all thy soul, and with all thy mind. (Mt 22:37)

[36] https://www.paulpearsall.com/info/press/3.html

[37] Paul Pearsall. The Heart's Code: Tapping the Wisdom and Power of Our Heart Energy (New York: Broadway Books, 1999).

tries to prove that when a certain but not necessarily sizable ratio of the population combine to meditate there is a drop in violence. Gregg Braden, a spokesperson for HMI and a YouTuber, suggests using a directed meditation of the heart which focuses on feelings of "appreciation, compassion, care, and gratitude." Gregg Braden - The Quantum Language of Healing, Peace & Miracles:

https://www.youtube.com/watch?v=rUVt650GdEI&t=426s

I consider my wife, who works as a crisis intervention worker, to be adept at heart consciousness. She can relate to the person in crisis with empathy, feel love for them, and have an intuitive and concrete appreciation for their state. She has an ability to recognize the innate value of the human being. She provides encouragement and possibilities to enable them to see their choices and opportunities.

I hope to have illustrated that we have an innate sense of the potential of the divine within us. For most of us humans this seems like a far-fetched reality. We are left with the idea of deism, that God (or some other impersonal natural force) created the world and then left it to us to sort it out. Isaiah reiterates, (to return to the notion that we are made in His image) "To whom then will ye liken God? or what likeness דמות will ye compare unto him?" (Isa 40:18) We are ultimately confronted with God, the indefinable. And yet He has blazed a trail for us, in the lives of those who have gone before. Many souls have inspired a hope within us, to reinvigorate our appreciation that we are intimately connected with a far greater reality. When I walk in the hallway of the Montreal General's 6th floor I am always moved by the tribute to John McCrae. "To you from failing hands we throw / The torch; be yours to hold it high." In the near future, our accelerated understanding of ultimate reality will give us a more coherent sense of what our relationship to our Creator implies.[38]

Thanks to the human heart by which we live,
Thanks to its tenderness, its joys, and fears,
To me the meanest flower that blows and gives
Thoughts that do often lie too deep for tears.[39]

Originally published in *The Montreal Review* in June 2023

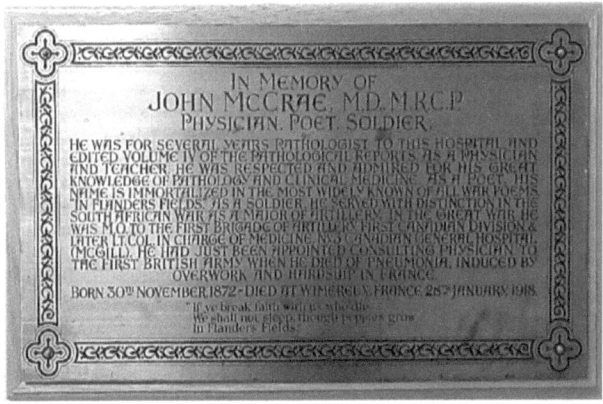

Figure 4: Memorial to Dr. John McCrae at the
Montreal General Hospital
In Memory of
John McCrae M.D. M.R.C.P.
Physician, Poet, Soldier.

---

[38] https://www.themontrealreview.com/Articles/Let_Us_Make_Man_in_Our_Image.php
[39] Wordsworth, William. *Intimations of Immortality*. The Poetical Works of William Wordsworth. Oxford University Press. p. 462, lines 204-207. First published 1903, 1953.

He was for several years pathologist to this hospital and edited Volume IV of the Pathological Reports. As a Physician and teacher, he was respected and admired for his great knowledge of pathology and clinical medicine. As a poet, his name is immortalized in the most widely known of all war poems, "In Flanders Fields." As a Soldier, he served with distinction in the South African War as a major of Artillery. In the Great War he was M.O. to the First Brigade of Artillery, First Canadian Division & later Lt. Col. in charge of medicine, N° 3 Canadian General Hospital (McGill). He had just been appointed Consulting Physician to the First British Army when he died of pneumonia, induced by overwork and hardship in France.

Born 30th November, 1872 - Died at Wimereux, France 28th January, 1918.
"If ye break faith with us who die,
We shall not sleep, thou poppies grow
In Flanders Fields."

A Male Bias in the New Testament?

The reliability of the transmitted text of the Bible, both the Old and New testaments has been authenticated more than any other historical document. The New Testament has more than 5,000 copies,[40] portions of, or complete texts of the Gospels and the Epistles. The Old Testament had a very reliable system of transmission, such that there were very few word changes between the newly discovered Dead Sea Scrolls found in 1946, and the oldest Masoretic texts. An example is the Isaiah Scroll from the Dead Sea Scrolls. Compared to the earliest Masoretic text, the Leningrad Codex, which was transcribed in 1008 AD,[41] there were minimal word differences. That is a time interval of approximately 1200 years between 1008 AD and the 3rd century BC, the publication date of the Scrolls. For a hand copied document to maintain internal integrity for over a millennium, shows incredible attention to accuracy and reliability.

So, compared to any other historical document[42] the recorded account and transmission of the New

---

[40] There are handwritten copies of the NT existing long before the age of printing, which in terms of quantity, exceed any other historical record. The date of some of the documents corresponds almost contemporaneously to the actual events if we are basing an argument on historical authenticity. Many of the texts, the Received Texts, are in general agreement amongst themselves.

[41] Leningrad Codex B19^A 1008 AD is published as the Biblia Hebraica Stuttgartensia, 1997.

[42] I.E., compared to the writings of Plato from 400 BC, the earliest copy of Plato is from 900 AD. The time from author to publication 1200 years, and there are seven copies. Another example are the writings of Caesar 44 BC. The

Testament as well as the Old Testament text is many times more reliable. The question here is whether there was male editorial bias.

I believe that a faithful reading of the Bible can inspire and lead us to a closer understanding of the Creator. If we listen with a sincere heart all that we need is available to us through God's word. "For the word of God is living and powerful, and sharper than any two-edged sword." (Heb 4:12a) We also know that there are many other things that Jesus did and said that are not recorded. (John 21:25)

However, and more recently, other texts have been found that lend a more nuanced interpretation to Christ's words. An unfortunate dilemma is the paucity of texts which when compared to the abundance of NT canonical texts, forces us to rely on unique examples. However, I suggest that a heartfelt reading of any text can allow us to perceive the legitimate intent of the author however subjective the interpretation. The most significant emphasis or lack of, is the role of women in the New Testament which appears to have been edited out by the largely male evangelical initiative which occupied the early centuries. This is a concern because for millennia the female voice has been obscured. Today, in the 21st century there is still widespread female subjugation both in secular and religious institutions.[43]

Recent examples of non-canonical texts are *The Unknown Life of Jesus Christ* by Nicolas Notovitch, or

---

earliest copy is from 900 AD. A total of 1000 years. Number of copies, 10.

[43] In a very unusual and chivalrous account the captain of the sinking ship HMS Birkenhead, commanded his soldiers to stand at attention while he ordered the "Women and children first." (1852) The soldiers remained at attention while the women and children were lowered to the boat. Approximately 450 soldiers were lost at sea. Some survived by swimming the two miles to shore.

La Vie inconnue de Jésus-Christ, published in Paris, by Paul Ollendorff, 1894. Notovich was a Russian, Crimean, Jewish explorer and journalist who visited the Himalayas in 1887. He reported on the existence of writings which claimed that Jesus had visited the monasteries of Tibet during his unknown years. There may also be texts by Mary Magdalene written while she lived in la Grotte de la Sainte Baume, France. She was buried in the nearby town of Saint-Maximin. There are possibly little-known writings available which may require some research, such as in the Vatican Library. Mary Magdalene was probably very well educated.[44] She appears to be the author of the *Gospel According to Mary* and has a significant voice in other Gnostic texts. In the *Pistis Sophia* she is the principal questioner of Jesus.

The *Papyrus Berolinensis* 8502 is a Coptic manuscript from the 5th century AD which includes *The Gospel According to Mary*, very likely Mary Magdalene. Again, there are no other copies that we know of that provide us with a comparable witness. However, the interaction described between Mary, Andrew, Peter, and Levi (a.k.a. Matthew)[45] testifies to the dynamic between the men and women in Christ's assembly. The conversation provides us with some insight into the culture of the Apostles at that time. In answer to Peter's request for a deeper understanding of a personal exchange between Jesus and Mary, Mary relates to the apostles a profound insight into the relation between soul, spirit, mind, and body. In fact, in encouraging the apostles Mary says, "He has made us into men," ...[46] suggesting that the

---

[44] In The Chosen One, Angel Studios, Mary is said to have learned to read from her father. :)

[45] See Mark 2:14.

[46] Gospel According to Mary, Papyrus Berolinensis, section 9, line 20.

promulgation of the Gospel has made both men and women more assertive. Peter and Andrew are not happy with Mary's understanding of Jesus' words even though they had previously asked her for an account into something that was communicated privately. This is the conversation:

> When Mary had said this, she fell silent, since it was to this point that the Savior had spoken with her. But Andrew answered and said to the brethren, say what you wish to say about what she has said. I at least do not believe that the Savior said this. For certainly these teachings are strange ideas. Peter answered and spoke concerning these same things. He questioned them about the Savior: Did He really speak privately with a woman and not openly to us? Are we to turn about and all listen to her? Did He prefer her to us? Then Mary wept and said to Peter, My brother Peter, what do you think? Do you think that I have thought this up myself in my heart, or that I am lying about the Savior? Levi answered and said to Peter, Peter you have always been hot tempered. Now I see you contending against the woman like the adversaries. But if the Savior made her worthy, who are you indeed to reject her? Surely the Savior knows her very well. That is why He loved her more than us. Rather let us be ashamed and put on the perfect Man, and separate as He commanded us and preach the gospel, not laying down any other rule or other law beyond what the Savior said. And when they heard this they

began to go forth to proclaim and to preach.[47]

The exchange between Mary, Peter, Andrew, and Levi provides a much more intimate account into the relations between them. We appreciate them as human beings. It is a conversation that helps us understand the interplay between the characters and sensitizes us to the dynamics they experienced. Some would read a sexual relationship into it; however, Jesus asked us to love everyone, including our enemies, it doesn't mean we should read more into it.

In the *Unknown Life* there are several deviations from the New Testament text, among them the decision by Pilate to pursue the prosecution of Christ, and the reluctance of the Jewish judges to be involved. This perspective on the trial of Jesus would probably have avoided much of the anti-Semitic policies since that time. The most important insight from The Unknown Life is the emphasis on the role of women which contrasts with Paul's statement in 1 Corinthians 14:34–35. Paul says, "Women should remain silent in the churches, they are not allowed to speak, but must be in submission." This is a difficult statement, and it is hard to understand whether it is a cultural reflection of the time or a priestly admonition.

Jesus (in contrast to Paul's statement) did not minimize the role of women. Compared to any other biblical figure he is by far the most interactive and engaging. He included women in his discipleship and possibly apostleship, (Mary Magdelene). He defends the woman condemned to be stoned by a very singularly minded group of men. "Neither do I condemn you; go and sin no more." (John 8:10–11) In the

---

[47] *Gospel According to Mary*, Papyrus Berolinensis, last section.

account of the woman at the well (John 4:7–26), Jesus' meeting with the Samaritan woman would have been considered culturally inappropriate at the time. Jesus encounters many women. The widow of Nain (Luke 7:12–13), the bleeding woman (Matt. 9:22; Mark 5:34; Luke 8:48), a woman in the crowd (Luke 11:27–28), a bent over woman on whom he lays his hands (Luke 13:12). He publicly honours the poor widow who contributes the two mites. (Mark 12:42, Luke 21:2). When Mary offered the sacrifice of spikenard, he defended her against the objections of 'some' (Mark), or Judas (John). (Mark 14:3; John 12:3). Women were the first to report on the resurrection. Donald G. Bloesch infers that "Jesus called the Jewish women 'daughters of Abraham' (Luke 13:16), thereby according them a spiritual status equal to that of men."[48] [49] Jesus affirmed women as persons having the fullest right to identity, freedom, and responsibility.[50] [51] Ben Witherington III writes, "Jesus broke with both biblical and rabbinic traditions that restricted women's roles in religious practices, and that He rejected attempts to devalue the worth of a woman, or her word of witness."[52] Jesus' position towards women is at odds with many contemporary religious positions of today. While he hung dying on the cross, he was concerned for the

---

[48] Donald G. Bloesch, Is the Bible Sexist? Beyond Feminism and Patriarchalism. Westchester, IL: Crossway Books, 1982. 5

[49] Borland, James A. Women in the Life and Teachings of Jesus. http://digitalcommons.liberty.edu/sor_fac_pubs

[50] John Paul II. The Dignity and Genius of Women. Love & Responsibility Foundation, Cold Spring, NY October 2003.

[51] https://www.vatican.va/content/john-paul-ii/en/letters/1995/documents/hf_jp-ii_let_29061995_women.html

[52] Witherington, Ben III. Women in the Ministry of Jesus, https://biblicalstudies.org.uk/pdf/ashland_theological_journal/17-1_22.pdf p. 28

care of his mother. (John 19:26–27) He said to John "behold your mother." "From that time the disciple took her to his own home." This is an incredibly thoughtful response by someone who is in extreme agony.

In Notovich's *The Unknown Life*, a witness from presumably a short time after the resurrection of Christ relates the following. In this account Jesus is being challenged by spies who were sent by Pilate to question his loyalty to Rome. This also reinforces the notion that, compared to the Jewish priests, Pilate was actively engaged in removing any threat to power:[53]

> At this point, an aged woman, who had approached the group that she might better hear Issa[54] (Jesus), was pushed aside by one of the men in disguise who placed himself before her. Issa then said: "It is not meet (i.e., right) that a son should push aside his mother to occupy the first place which should be hers. Whosoever respecteth not his mother, the most sacred being next to God, is unworthy the name of son."
>
> "Listen, therefore, to what I am about to say: "Respect woman, for she is the mother of the universe and all the truth of divine creation dwells within her." "She is the basis of all that is good and beautiful, as she is also the germ of life and death. On her depends the entire

---

[53] Notovich, *The Unknown Life of Jesus Christ*, identified as verses 8-21. Indo-American Book Company, 5705 South Boulevard, Chicago, ILL. Fourth Edition, Ch. XII, pp. 136-138, 1916.

[54] Issa is also the Muslim name for Jesus.

existence of man, for she is his moral and natural support in all his works."

"She gives you birth amid sufferings; by the sweat of her brow she watches over your growth, and until her death you cause her the most intense anguish. Bless her and adore her, for she is your only friend and support upon earth," "Respect her, protect her; in doing this, you will win her love and her heart, and you will be pleasing to God; for this shall many of your sins be remitted." "Therefore, love your wives and respect them, for to-morrow they shall be mothers, and later grandmothers of a whole nation." "Be submissive toward your wife; her love ennobles man, softens his hardened heart, tames the beast and makes of it a lamb."

"The wife and the mother, inestimable treasures bestowed on you by God; they are the most beautiful ornaments of the universe, and from them shall be born all that shall inhabit the world. Just as the God of armies separated day from night and the land from the waters, so woman possesses the divine talent of separating good intentions from evil thoughts in men."

Therefore, I say to you: "After God, your best thoughts should belong to women and to wives; woman being to you the divine temple wherein you shall most easily obtain perfect happiness." "Draw your moral strength from this temple; there you will forget your sorrows and failures, you will recover the wasted forces necessary to help your neighbor." "Do not expose her to humiliation; you would thereby humiliate yourself and lose the sentiment of love, without which nothing exists here below." "Protect your wife, that she may protect you and all your family; all that you shall do for your mother, your wife, for a widow, or another woman in distress, you shall have done for God."

In the Tibetan archival account Jesus not only affirms women, he also criticizes the religious hierarchical system. So, it is not just a purely Eastern take on a Western philosophy, it appears to be a legitimate record of a close witness to Christ. It is an extraordinarily deep appreciation of the role of women.

The text provides a much more valuable and appreciative account of Jesus' view. A very legalistic interpretation might suggest that there are discrepancies compared to the canonical text. However, a sincere reading can sensitize our hearts and help us appreciate a very endearing description of women. The text points out the significant difference of the treatment of women as recorded by the canonical NT text and quite possibly what was said by Jesus. So, was there a bias by the first apostles in the early witness? Were the testimonies of Mary Magdalene excluded from the earliest texts?

The suppression of women has existed for millennia. There were protests and publications during the French Revolution beginning in 1789, however the Seneca Falls Convention in New York state was apparently the first women's rights convention. It was held in 1848. John Stuart Mill published his *The Subjection of Women* in 1869 arguing for the equality of the sexes. The first suffragette parades were held in Britain in 1907, and in 1908 up to 500,000 attended. In 1913 a civil rights march on Washington included five thousand participants. By the end of the protest at least 100 people were injured.[55] According to Gloria Steinem, gender equality movements were practiced within the Haudenosaunee (Iroquois) nations long before America was colonized.[56] There have been significant changes in our cultures, hard fought by women at a high cost. It is true that women are still being disrespected, under recognized as skilled leaders, insulted, and abused in workplaces, homes, and churches. We could conclude that many church bodies are influenced by these early texts as they continue to be sidelined in church leadership and some denominations are entirely male dominated. Let us get back to Gods original intent - The garden.

Rather than moving forward with a better appreciation of the female, the English Standard Version, the ESV[57] appears to be moving backwards. Samuel L. Perry's, *The Bible as a Product of Cultural Power*,[58] describes instances where the role of women has been downgraded. In an important passage regarding the fate of all women the RSV (Revised Standard Version) reads, "your desire shall be for your husband, and he shall rule over you".

---

[55] https://guides.loc.gov/american-women-essays/marching-for-the-vote accessed October 15, 2023

[56] Wagner, Sally Roesch; Steinem, Gloria (2019). The Women's Suffrage Movement (1st ed.). New York, New York: Penguin Books. pp. 1, 45–49, 75, 82, 356–7. ISBN 978-0-525-50441-2

[57] The Revised Standard Version, the RSV 1952, and the ESV (Crossway, 2016)

[58] Perry, Samuel L. The Bible as a Product of Cultural Power: The Case of Gender Ideology in the English Standard Version. Sociology of Religion: A Quarterly Review 2020, 81:1 68–92

(Genesis 3:16b) The ESV (Crossway, 2016) reads, "Your desire shall be contrary to your husband, but he shall rule over you." A confrontational revision putting the male and female completely at odds with each other.

My wife worked in conjugal violence for several years[59] and at times worked with women who were part of a church community. When she and the woman suffering the abuse turned to the pastor for support for what the woman was experiencing, she was usually advised to stay in the marriage. Submission was expected even if there was ongoing violence.

In the Catholic tradition the Virgin Mary is highly venerated. She is very rightly held in an honourable position to which women may sometimes be compared.[60] However, there are very few female role models other than Martha and Mary and heroines of the Old Testament. There is very little conversational interaction between Jesus and women. The male apostles come across as normal humans with all their character flaws. However, in the statement allegedly by Jesus in Notovich's account women are given their rightful place. The focus on the woman, the honour he shows her, restores the value that is inherent to the nature of womanhood and not some idealized quality to which she may sometimes be held to.

The vision of the two witnesses in Revelation 11 is a very enigmatic picture. It is comparable to the vision of Zachariah 4. The witnesses could be two individuals. Or, to speculate further, were these

---

[59] The Friendly Home. *Adventures with God and Little People.* Roulson, Olive. (Montreal, 1988). This account was published while the Home was a shelter for unwed mothers. In the 1990s it became a shelter for women enduring conjugal violence.

[60] On a separate and very oblique historical note, it is said that: "When England returns to Walsingham, Our Lady will return to England. https://walsinghamcommunity.org/

witnesses a representation of the Old and New Testaments. Or are they representative of the people of the Jews and the Christians? However, another possibility presents itself. Are the witnesses a vision of the male and female. Will the original family of creation (as ourselves) return in complete harmony? To quote Genesis 2: 24-25, "Therefore a man shall leave his father and mother and be joined to his wife, and they shall become one flesh. And they were both naked, the man and his wife, and were not ashamed." In the very next verse, in Genesis 3:1 the serpent steps in. It is ultimately up to us, as men and women to reconcile the original differences in Creation and to take ownership of our true nature. To quote Joni Mitchell. "We are stardust / We are golden / And we got to get ourselves / Back to the garden / We are star dust / Billion year old carbon / We are golden / Caught in the devil's bargain / And we got to get ourselves back to the garden."[61]

Originally published in *The Montreal Review* in April 2024. The article for the Male Bias and the New Testament was reviewed by Dr. Christine Jamieson, in the Department of Theological Studies at Concordia University. Dr. Jamieson is the author of *Christian Ethics and the Crisis of Gender Violence*. Stephen's wife, Wendy Mellor Machnik, helped with input and editing of the text. Wendy works at Tracom, a crisis centre in Montreal, as a crisis intervention worker from 2003 to the present (2024). Prior to Tracom she worked at the Friendly Home a shelter for women suffering marital abuse in the early 90s. Lynn Beaudin, the director of the Friendly Home at that time also provided input. Wendy was a dancer and danced with

---

[61] Mitchell, Joni. *Woodstock*. Ladies of the Canyon.

Canada's Les Feux Follets in the 60s. (https://www.thecanadianencyclopedia.ca/en/article/les-feux-follets)

www.ingramcontent.com/pod-product-compliance
Lightning Source LLC
Chambersburg PA
CBHW030555080526
44585CB00012B/379